The

Money

Field

Book 3

Nelson Letshwene

Nelson Letshwene

How to Pay Off Your Debt and Build Wealth

,

Nelson Letshwene

How to Pay Off Your Debts and Build Wealth -

Avoiding The Trap of Other People's Money

Nelson Letshwene

Published by
Moedi Publishing, a division of Moedi Learning Technologies.
PO Box 80927, Gaborone, Botswana.
PO Box 1766, Rustenburg, 0323
Pretoria, South Africa

©R. Nelson Letshwene
nelslets@gmail.com / nelson@moedi.net
www.nelsonletshwene.com
Moedi Publishing
ISBN: 978-0-9870189-7-7

KDP Assigned ISBN:
9798701487701

Nelson Letshwene

"A man in debt is so far a slave"

Ralph Waldo Emerson

DISCLAIMER:

This publication is designed to provide competent and reliable general information regarding the subject matter covered. However, it is published with the understanding that the author and publisher are not engaged in rendering legal, financial, or other professional advice. If legal, financial, or other expert assistance is required, the services of a professional should be sought. The author and publisher specifically disclaim any liability that is incurred from the use or application of the contents of this book.

Nelson Letshwene

Other books by Nelson Letshwene: Books in The Money Field Series:

1. Book One: The Money Field - How to Set Your Own Money Rules
2. Book Two: Money Goals and Money Management Tools – Practical Strategies for Living in the Gap
3. Book Three: How to Pay Off Your Debts and Build Wealth – Avoiding The "Trap" of Other People's Money

To get access to other books by this author, Visit www.amazon.com/R-Nelson-Letshwene/e/B00Q4AEMCM/ref

Or Scan the QR Code

Table of Contents

Nelson Letshwene

INTRODUCTION TO BOOK 3

"Creditors have better memories than debtors"

Benjamin Franklin

This three-book series has covered The Money Game, Strategies for Living In the Gap, and now comes to "The Trap of Other People's Money", or Debt Management Systems.

While it would be beneficial to read the first two books in the series, the topic of this book is also a stand-alone topic and you can learn a whole lot by just understanding the subject of debt on its own merit.

The first book in *The Money Field Series*, *How to Set Your Own Money Rules – Mastering the Money Game*, covers the concept of the four quadrants of the money field upon which the game of money is played.

Of course, the second book in the series, *Money Goals and Money Management Tools*, covers life in the gap between the setting of your goals and achieving them – the activities you must do that will lead you to reaching your goals.

This third book in the series, How to Pay Off your Debts and Building Wealth – Avoiding *the Trap of Other People's Money*, mainly focuses on the one quadrant that makes up the Liabilities quadrant.

To understand the other quadrants of The Money Field, it would be important to read the other two books in the series.

We focus on debt in this book only because it is one of the biggest traps that stop people from focusing on the number one goal of building wealth by growing their assets. Debt has a potential to eat away not only at your valuable time of building wealth, but also at the assets you have already gathered.

While the expenses quadrant is where lifestyle can be changed, the liabilities quadrant is a double-edged sword.

In the hands of the financially illiterate, debt can be a dangerous tool to use. In the hands of the financially literate, it can be a helpful tool. It is important to understand this subject on its own merit.

I hope this book will add value to the life of the reader, and help to increase financial literacy and other money skills that are so important in our lives today.

If you find this book helpful, please feel free to give us some feedback or leave us a review.

Thank you,

Nelson Letshwene

January, 2021
Gaborone, Botswana
nelson@moedi.net

PREFACE

"Neither a lender nor a borrower be"

William Shakespeare

Debt has been said to be an opportunity for the rich. What it implies for the poor is that it is a risk.

The rich use other people's money to build their wealth. It is not a trap for them because they set in place systems to ensure that the borrowed money can return safely to the lender.

The problem with the poor is that they borrow money for consumption. Once consumed, they have to work hard to repay the debt. They have no systems that repay the debt. It is their own sweat and blood that they have to engage to repay the debt. These are those that often need help to get out of oppressive debt. Wisdom is required when you deal with debt.

The purpose of this book is to give such wisdom. Get an understanding of how to use debt and, if you find yourself entangled, understand the processes of freeing yourself from the trap.

.

Chapter 1

1. Why Do People Want to Lend You Their Money?

"Opportunity is missed by most people because it is dressed in overalls and looks like work."
Thomas Edison

Why is it that so much of the world is eager to get their money into your pocket?

The World Bank and the International Monetary Fund (IMF) are trying to get their money into the pockets of countries around the world. Banks are trying to get their money into the pockets of businesses around the globe.

Financial institutions that used to focus only on your protection like Insurance companies, are now in the lending space, eager to get their money into your pockets. Mind you, this is the same money that you have contributed to them as your premiums for protection. Now they want you to borrow it.

Banks and other financial institutions have intensified their marketing efforts to get you to borrow their money. Micro lending organizations are popping up everywhere.

Even if you are already in debt, many companies are still eager to have you put *their* money into *your* pockets.

What is in your pocket that so many institutions would like to get their money there? What do they see in there that you do not see?

There are really two important things that the world of lenders would like to take from you: your earning potential and your assets. If your earning potential can make other people rich over time, why would you not use it to your own advantage?

Graduates don't have assets other than their earning potential. Lenders load them up with loans so that over their life time, they can labour for these financial institutions.

Those who have assets have collateral, and lenders would like to get their claws on these hard-earned assets.

Countries with natural resources get loaded

up with World Bank and IMF loans and end up losing not only their resources over time, these institutions even use the country's labour resources to get their money out. They claim they are creating jobs, but people work for them to get the country's resources out. These people end up poor at the end of their lives because even they are loaded up with personal debt.

In John Perkins[1]'s book, we learn of dirty secrets of how the world would like to own your resources.

If you are caught in this web of other people's money, it is important that you free yourself as early as you can.

This book teaches you the tools of debt or instruments used to bring other people's money into your pockets. It goes on to show you the structure of debt, or what the trap is made up of so that you can disentangle yourself easily. It then discusses strategies for eliminating debt and staying out of debt, thus keeping your own money working for

---

[1] John Perkins, *Confessions of an Economic Hit Man*, Penguin, 2004

you, instead of it working for other people.

You have enough resources over your lifetime to make yourself wealthy. You do not need to be in a hurry to take other people's money. You need to be smart enough to employ your own money and resources to enrich your own life.

I hope this instalment of the third book in The Money Field Series will enlighten you and help you to take charge of your economic power.

Chapter 2

2. Other People's Money

"Do not spit in the well – you may be thirsty by and by".
Russian Proverb

LEARNING OUTCOMES
In this chapter you will learn:
- The role of legal persons in perpetuating debt
- The necessity of Debt
- When does debt go wrong?

Before we talk about other people's money, it may be helpful to talk about our own money. Our world is run on the principle of cause and effect. You reap what you sow. You cannot reap more than you have sowed. Our own money, more often than not, come to us as a result of the sale of our own skills, talents, capabilities, and energies in the market place to willing employers.

There is a saying that "there ain't no such thing as a free lunch". Our money is a reward for trading in the market place. It seems therefore that life is a process of trading one thing for another.

Once we have traded our own energies and have acquired money, we in turn go and trade the money in the market place for goods and services, according to our needs, wants, and desires.

When we run out of money in the market place, we go back to sell more of our energies to acquire more money so that we can go back in the market place to acquire more goods and services.

As long as each one only trades as much money as they are able to make through their energies, the system seems to stay in balance.

The problem begins when I start wanting more goods and services now, than my hard-earned money can acquire right now. This is when I start employing, other people's money.

When I use other people's money today, money I have not yet earned, I am making a promise to them that I will devote a portion of my energies, skills, talents, capabilities, tomorrow, to earn their money for them.

Unfortunately, they inform me, that tomorrow, the prices of goods and services will be higher than today. So, if I use their money today, I must be willing to bring back tomorrow's money, which is higher than today's money.

Hoping that the price of my labour will be higher tomorrow, I agree and sign on the dotted line. I remain indebted to the money lender until I can pay him all of tomorrow's money. If the price of my labour does not go up as I had hoped, I start to fall behind.

Debt, is nothing but other people's money. Other people's money is other people's energies, skills, talents, and capabilities.

Unfortunately, or fortunately, depending on how you look at it, we have created on our planet, "legal persons" who do not have flesh and blood like natural persons.

These participate in the money market just like natural persons, and they obviously have an unfair advantage. They don't get tired, hungry, thirsty, sleepy, or even old. Some of them specialize in "manufacturing" money, and lending it out to natural persons.

You have to be very careful and very smart when you play the money game with these "people". A bank is a legal entity. It is not a human being. It will not get tired. It will not get old. But you will. Yes, it employs natural people, who get old and retire, and it employs more, who get old and retire, and so on and so forth. Even the CEO will get old and retire, and a new one will sit at the helm, and the process goes on.

So, you can't get emotional when you are playing the money game with an entity that has no emotions. You must seek to understand its language, and speak that language.

If, in the unlikely event that the bank should owe you - a natural person - money, it can just "manufacture" it and pay you off. I know that sounds very simplistic. But the fact that the bank can lend more money than it actually has, is proof that the bank can "manufacture" money. But that is a topic for another day.

For those interested in the banking system, there are many books on the subject, including *The Creature from Jekyll Island*[2], by Edward Griffin.

Now, back to the subject at hand.

The Necessity of Debt

Is debt really that necessary? Can we really live without debt?

Banks and lending institutions have a big role to play in the development of our economies and societies. Without them rolling out debt, a lot of industrialists would not be able to innovate, invent, and improve lives.

Think of an industrialist like Henry Ford. If the banks did not advance him the money to build a motor manufacturing factory, we would still be walking or riding donkeys to work.

If the banks did not advance loans to General Electric, we would still be burning wood for light. If textile manufacturers had not

---

[2] Griffin, G. Edward, 1994, The Creature from Jekyll Island, American Media

borrowed money, we would still be running barefoot and topless. If there was no money lent to Microsoft, Apple and Google, we would still be whistling and shouting at each other to get each other's attention.

So yes, debt is necessary.

Without debt individuals would not be able to own homes at the rate that they can with debt. They would not be able to drive and own cars and furniture. They would not be able to pay for their children's education, which is an important investment in the future of their offspring.

When Does Debt Go Out of Hand?

Business debt goes wrong when it is given to incompetent entrepreneurs who confuse business money with personal money. Debt goes out of hand when it is given to people who cannot afford it. It goes out of hand when individuals start depending on it for survival. It goes out of hand when it is used for consumables like food and clothing. It goes out of hand when individuals use their houses like ATMs, cashing their equity for consumables. It goes wrong when there are no proper standards for measuring the adequacy of debt for each household.

It goes wrong when financial institutions are disconnected from each other and are not communicating with each other about each client. It would be good if they had a central system where they can check each client before they advance the money. Not just the credit bureau, which keeps a record of black listed people, but a system which can check the adequacy of debt per individual before the loans are advanced.

Generally, debt goes wrong in the hands of people who have no financial education, and cannot distinguish between their own money and other people's money, and their abilities to repay loans.

As long as we use money on our planet, debt is not going to disappear. It is too important for enabling developments. What we need therefore are better systems of managing debt. We need a financially educated society from business to individuals. We need legislation and supportive systems from government.

Yes, debt is important, but education about

debt and money is even more important.

SELF-ASSESSMENT 1

1. What is the implication of using other people's money?

2. How do other players influence my money game?

3. What are the reasons that make debt necessary?

4. What would be the consequences if there was no debt?

5. When does debt go wrong?

Chapter 3

3. Tools of Debt

The borrower is servant to the lender.
Proverbs 22:7

LEARNING OUTCOMES
In this chapter you will learn:
1.   The difference between secured debt and unsecured debt.
2.   Various tools of credit
3.   The Use and misuse of tools of credit
4.   The importance of credit life insurance
5.   The importance of cash as king

If you borrow money, and your goal is not to employ it but to consume it, then the proverb above applies. You have become a slave to the lender. You will work until you pay the last penny, including interest. If you fail, then your personal belongings will be sold to recover the debt.

Industrialists and business people don't borrow the bank's money to consume it, but to employ it. They speak the language of the bank. I believe if the bank had its way, it would only lend money to such people; people who would employ money. This guarantees the bank that it will get its money back.

The bank plays the game of the rich. It employs money. The most important employee of the bank, the hardest worker, is money; not the teller behind the counter, but the money in her hands. The teller draws a salary at the end of the month and is therefore an expense to the bank. The teller is dispensable, but not the cash. The bank's job is to send its money out to work and make more money for it.

If the bank could do everything through the Automated Teller Machine, they would do that. It would be cheaper for them.

The machine does not need a salary, it doesn't go on strike, and it does not take a coffee break, just regular maintenance is enough.

Now, the bank has created tools, or products, which it can sell to borrowers. The borrower is the garden on which the bank will plant its seed, hoping to reap a plentiful harvest. They will not plant their seed on barren land. You must learn to harness the power of debt.

Here are some of the tools of credit or products created by financial institutions for various clients:

1. Business loans
2. Mortgage loans
3. Personal loans
4. Short term asset loans (e.g., car loan/furniture)
5. Credit cards
6. Overdraft facilities

Let us explain them each briefly. Before we go into the explanations, let us understand the most important thing to a lender, before they lend their money out, is a certain level of certainty that they will be able to get their money back. This leads to secured loans and unsecured loans.

Secured vs. unsecured debt

What is secured debt?

Secured debt is debt that has collateral backing it up. This is a trade. The lender is willing to lend you money, but in the event that you fail to repay the loan, you have some assets that they can take and sell and get their money back. You pledge these assets to the lender before they can give you a loan.

What is unsecured debt.

Unsecured debt is the opposite. This is a loan that has no collateral backing it up. When the bank talks of security, it is talking about its own security, not yours. They feel secure if they lend money to someone who has assets, and they feel insecure if they are lending to someone who has no assets. To compensate for this insecurity, the bank charges the highest interest on unsecured loans.

Tools of Debt

Now let us briefly look at each of the tools of credit. There is more to each of these than the brief descriptions given here.

It would be prudent to do more research if you would like to utilise any of these, or seek deeper understanding.

1. The Business loan

A business loan is given to a business that can show, in various ways, including through its business plan that it will generate the money to repay the loan. The business will get a secured loan if they have assets that they can pledge to the bank. In the event that the business does not produce the revenues that allow it to service the loan, the bank can seize and sell the assets of the business to recover its money.

2. Mortgage Loan

Generally, a mortgage loan is a loan

advanced to a person or company that wants to buy or build a piece of real estate property. It may also be given as "equity release" to one who already has such a property that has value that the bank can mortgage.

The property is mortgaged to the bank as security. Should the borrower fail to repay the loan, the bank could sell the piece of real estate to recover its money. This is called a secured loan by the bank. Security, of course, to the bank.

We have a full chapter on how to pay off your mortgage in record time later on in this book (Chapter 9)

3. Personal Loans

Personal loans are unsecured loans based on the borrower's earning capabilities, which is often based mostly on employment. Your payslip gives you borrowing capacity. Since the lender depends on nothing else but your salary, they tend to charge a high interest for this facility.

The bank doesn't care what you use this money for. There is no particular asset attached to this loan. But don't assume that if you fail to repay the loan, the bank will not take your other assets to sell to recover their money.

4. Short term asset finance loans

Other secured loans include car loans and furniture loans based on the hire purchase scheme.

The car remains the bank's asset until you finish paying for it; just like the furniture on a hire-purchase scheme remain the property of the furniture shop until you finish paying for it.

5. Credit cards

Credit cards are essentially the bank giving you a line of credit for a certain amount of time, usually two years. During this period, you may use the bank's money to the extent of your credit limit. Your responsibilities are to pay the minimum amounts as calculated by the bank.

What you have to remember about credit cards is that as long as you are only paying the minimum amount, you will be charged interest on any remaining amount unpaid at the end of the month. Be aware that if you only pay the minimum balance, you will almost never get out of this debt, even if you never use the credit card again. Remember that the monthly interest levied is as if you charged or used your credit card, and the bank treats that as a loan to you. The minimum repayment determined by the bank is the minimum on that interest charge (loan to you), plus the minimum on the other balance before they charged you interest. In essence they're lending you the money to pay them, and next month they will charge you interest on that.

If, however, you pay off all that you have used up before the interest charging day, you will be using the bank's money for free. So, if you don't want to pay interest on your credit card, you should never carry a balance.

6. Overdraft facilities

An overdraft facility is a line of credit extended to you by the bank, often tied to your transactional current or cheque account. When your own money runs out, you can continue to swipe your card, using the bank's money to the extent of the line of credit. You will be charged interest on any amount that you use. If you don't use it, you don't get charged any interest, but you may be charged a fee for the facility, whether you use it or not.

7. Store cards

Store cards are essentially a line of credit extended to you by retailers. Most clothing retailers have store cards that give you a credit limit. You can take clothes, for example, on credit and pay them over time.

This is not free money. You will be charged interest on any outstanding balance.

If an item is only 100.00 bucks, please understand that if you take it on credit, the price will go up by the amount of interest you will be charged.

If goods are "on sale" and have been discounted by say 10%, if you take them on credit, and the interest is 20%, know that you will be paying 110% for them.

Your alternative to store cards is of course cash, but if you can't afford that you could always layby or lay away and pay it over time, interest free.

Credit Life Insurance

Most credit cards and almost all secured and unsecured debt come with credit life insurance. Credit life mostly covers events such as death. Should you die before the loan is repaid, the insurance company undertakes to pay off the loan.

Some credit life may cover life events such as disability, and retrenchment under certain conditions. Whenever you take a loan, read your credit life insurance policy to make sure you understand what is covered and what is not covered.

The Use and Misuse of Tools of Debt

Being educated about debt is critically important. When banks create loan packages, they are looking at matching your needs with their needs.

If you don't know much about debt, you can mix up the packages and use wrong products.

For example, if you use a personal loan to build or buy a house, you are using a wrong product for your needs. The interest for a personal loan is very high because by its nature, a personal loan is an unsecured debt. The interest for a mortgage loan is low because the house is used as security.

It therefore does not make economic sense to use a very expensive personal loan to finance the building of a house, which you could have financed with cheap mortgage loan.

It further does not make economic sense to roll off personal loans and car loans into your mortgage through the process called debt consolidation.

Match your project needs with the right kind of debt.

Is Cash King?

Many financial teachers or advisors would have you believe that it is best to be a cash buyer and stay away from debt. And perhaps they are right. For a lot of people, operating a cash system has kept them out of unnecessary heartaches, and many more would do well to try the cash-is-king system. However, without debt, many desires would go unfulfilled. Some people feel they can't save up for 20 years to buy a house or for 5 years to buy a car. Debt allows them to have these things now. So, if it's available, and you can afford it, why not?

There are no right or wrong answers. There are only preferences. Whatever preferences you choose, be informed about them, and be well conversant with how they work. It is not the availability of debt that is a problem, it is the management of debt that gives people a lot of problems. It is important to have the guidance of a trained financial advisor to go through your specific situation.

In the next chapter we begin to look at the building blocks of debt, the four elements of debt.

SELF-ASSESSMENT 2

1.   What is the difference between secured debt and unsecured debt?

2.   List at least five tools of credit?

3.   Which of the tools of credit are most important to you and why?

4.   What is the importance of credit life insurance?

5.   How do consumers misuse tools of credit?

Chapter 4

4. The Four Elements of Debt

"Never spend your money before you have earned it."

Thomas Jefferson

LEARNING OUTCOMES

In this chapter you will learn;

1. The four elements of debt

2. The importance of co-ordinating the four elements of debt

3. The effects of isolating each of the elements of debt

Let us start by understanding the four very important elements of debt. Every loan or credit that you have taken is characterised by four elements: the principal amount, the instalment, interest, and time. These factors are inextricably intertwined and each one of them affects the others.

An increase in one of them affects the others, and a decrease in any one affects all the others. None of these are independent of each other. The danger that faces borrowers is that they don't see the relationship of each of these factors to each other, and as a result, treat them as separate entities. Let us look at each one of them at a time.

1. The Loan Amount

The loan amount is the total amount that you will owe the lender at the start of the loan. This is not to be confused with the amount that you receive in your account.

The amount you receive in your account will be the total loan, decreased by administration fees, credit life insurance, initiation fees, and whatever other fees your lender may charge you to arrive at the total amount of the loan.

Once the additional charges are computed,

they are subtracted from the amount of the loan to arrive at what you will receive in your account. The inverse can also be true, where, instead of subtracting from the loan, the charges are added to the loan, and you still only receive what you had hoped for, but you owe a lot more than what you received at the start of the loan. In other words, the lender also lends you money to cover the administration charges and whatever other charges there are.

If, for an example, you want to borrow 50'000, the total amount you owe will be affected by all the other factors.

If all additional fees add up to about 5'000, you will only receive 45'000 in your account.

If the *interest rate is 10% per annum compounded monthly over 2 years*, your instalments over the period will be 2'307.25.

You can see that if you multiplied your instalment amount by 24 months, you get 55'373.91. This is the total amount being owed. You only got 45'000 in your account, but you will sign that you owe the lender 55'373.91.

Most borrowers don't think about anything

else. All they want to know is: how much is coming into their hands right now. That is why others would insist on getting the 50'000 in their hands, and let the lender put additional charges on top.

---

2. The Instalment Amount

The next important thing that most borrowers worry about is: how much are the monthly instalments?

They are not looking at the total amount that the series of instalments will amount to. They only want to know if they can afford it this month!

Making a commitment today that has long term repercussions that you don't consider, is dangerous.

A person who is only worried about instalments, may say to the lender, please make my instalments easier.

In the above example, they might say, I can't afford to pay 2'307,91. Please make it easier for the instalments to fit into my monthly budget without reducing the size of the loan I'm taking home.

To make it "affordable", the lender might reduce instalments to 1'268,13. This might make the borrower happy. But the only way to reduce instalments to this level is to increase time to 4 years or 48 months.

Now, multiplying the 1'268,13 by 48 months makes the loan amount 60'870,20. You still only get 45'000 in your account, but your will repay a total of 60'870,20, which is 15'870,20 more! This happens when you only focus on instalments.

It is obviously very important to make sure that you can afford your instalments, but it is vitally important that you think about the whole picture.

The lower your instalments are, the longer you will take to repay the debt. The longer you take, the higher your principal debt.

3. Interest

Interest is the price you pay for borrowed money. Most borrowers have no clue what this really means. They understand the amount of the loan that is coming into their account, and they also understand the instalments they will pay every month. They however, have no clue how the concept called interest plays a role.

This is why most people can't differentiate between a loan taken from a bank and a loan taken from cash loan or loan sharks.

While the bank will quote their interest using annual rate, the loan shark uses monthly rate. An annual rate of 20% at the bank, and a monthly rate of 20% at the loan shark seem to be the same to an untrained and desperate borrower.

The bank's annual rate will most like be compounded monthly, which, in simplistic terms, means the 20% per annum will be divided by 12 months to give you a monthly rate of 1.67%.

Now, comparing this with the loan shark who will be charging the full 20% every month, where should you really go to go borrow money?

If you just multiplied the loan shark's 20% by 12 months, you will see that you are paying 240% per annum.

Each time you take a loan, consider the price you are paying for the loan. Money is not free. Money is sold in the money market at a price. You should get the most competitive price possible for your money.

When the bank says "you qualify" for a loan, they are not doing you a favour. They are also looking for customers. You don't have to sign on the spot. It is important that you should shop around and find the most affordable interest that you can afford.

There is nothing wrong with getting several quotations from several lenders to compare the terms before you make your decision.

People who go to loan sharks often say they do so because they don't qualify at the bank. Here is what does not make sense: if you don't qualify at the bank where the interest rates are lower, why would you take money where it is most expensive?

And the answer is, I'm under pressure. I need the money now.

Don't allow desperation to lead you into the most expensive loans. Remember, this is other people's money, and it comes at a price. Don't be in a hurry to take other people's money without considering what it will cost you.

4. Time

Time is a very fleeting factor in debt management and most people don't give it a second thought because they can't see it.

But by just looking at the example we used above, see what the difference in the loan amount is between a loan that is repaid in 2 years (24 months) and a loan that is repaid in 4 years (48 months).

Most people who consolidate their loans or do "top ups" only think about the pressure of the Instalment amount, and do not consider time or the interest rate.

Sometimes they only see the pressure of the problem in front of them that requires money. They go and borrow money to solve the "big" problem in front of them that require money, without considering that they are giving birth to an even bigger problem that will take years to resolve. Before you ever take a loan, think about these four elements of debt and how they will affect you.

Debt restructuring often focuses on reducing your instalments. But you must remember, for instalments to go down, it means time must go up. When time goes up, the principal amount goes up, simply because you will be paying your interest for longer.

SELF-ASSESSMENT 3

1. What are the four elements of debt?

2. Explain how each of the four elements of debt play a role in the composition of debt

3. What are the effects of isolating the four elements of debt from each other?

4. What happens if you only focus on reducing the monthly instalment to a loan?

5. Is Debt consolidation a good idea for you?

Chapter 5

5. The Gap Planning System

"When a man is in love or in debt, someone else has the advantage."
Bill Balance

LEARNING OUTCOMES

In this chapter you will learn:

1. How to set up a planning structure

2. The importance of protection in your structure

Here is the Financial Planning System I suggest. It is important to have your income statement and balance sheet in front of you so that you know what you are dealing with. The key with a planning system is that it must propel you forward instead of holding you at the same place or worse, taking you back.

Now you must determine the flow of your cash. What happens to money when it arrives into your system?

You need to watch it so that you can make decisions and perhaps redirect the flow of your cash if it is going the wrong way.

For most people, unfortunately the money does not even arrive into their hands. The pay-slip shows that the money gets taken from the employer by their creditors and only very little makes it to their pockets. So, they really have no control over the flow of their cash.

For other people, whereas the pay-slip may show that they get most of their money from the employer, the bank statement will show that the direct debits on their accounts are like blood suckers and they are still broke at the end of the pay period.

Now, the Planning System is based on a suggested 10:10:20:60 system. This is only a suggestion depending where you are at. If you can't apply this right away, you can make it your goal to achieve it in a set period of time. It is important to save 10% of your earnings. If you can't, keep making adjustments to your life until you reach this goal. You do the same with all the other allocations as explained below.

- The first 10% should go to Paying Yourself First. This money goes in an account and is not taken out until you are ready to invest it. A savings account is not necessarily an investment account. By investment I mean things like the money market, the stock market, mutual funds or unit trusts, real estate, your business, etc. This 10% is only to be applied to such investments, and not to other expenses. No one can build wealth unless a portion of their income goes towards building wealth. This portion is not emergency savings. It is wealth building savings.
- While Retirement funding is mentioned here seemingly in passing, it is a vital part of your future investments, that will ensure that you continue to have an income in your old age. Do not neglect it or pay lip service to it. Retirement funding may straddle between this first 10% and

the second 10%.

- The second 10% should at least go to Protection. Protection makes sure that the assets you are gathering are not exposed to vulnerabilities. If you have finished paying for your home, make sure you get homeowner insurance. This will protect your house against fire or other damages like a leaking geyser. If you don't have this cover, you might find yourself having to start over. Make sure all your assets are well insured. You should also have a good life insurance policy, Retirement annuity, and a rainy-day reserve or emergency fund

- Failure to have adequate life insurance can leave you in a desperate position should anything drastic happen. Some people claim they can't afford life insurance, but I believe that especially if you can't afford it, then you can't afford to be without it. Dealing with financial problems without a good life insurance cover is like going to war without protection.

- The next 20% of your income should be what is used to cover all your debts. If you are in big debts, you might be saying that is not possible! Pay attention for a while here. Take a list of all your debts and decide that you will only apply 20% of your income to repay them. Yes, this means you will have to call them and make new arrangements if you are already using much more than 20% to service debt. If this is not immediately possible, make it your goal to cut your debt servicing amount to only 20% or less. Take control of your cash flow. We will look at different methods in the next chapter.

- If you don't have a lot of debt to deal with, then focus this on your Retirement funding because that will also give you tax breaks.
- We allocate 60% to your current living expenses because it is important that you do not get in any more debt. You should be able to live without borrowing from the first day to the last day of the month. Most people stay in debt because they don't allocate enough of their own money to themselves. So, they are always dependent on debt for survival. To close

the door on debt starts with you not entering that door ever again.

If you can do this, you are on your way out of trouble. Avoid another "survival-till-end-of-the-month" loan.

That is why you need to allocate enough of your money to avoid the "lend-me-I'll-pay-at-month-end" syndrome.

It is worth emphasizing that if you want to get out of debt and start building a nest egg, it is important that you don't continue to get into any more debt – even if it is short term (especially unsecured debt).

You need to banish the idea and find other ways to survive. Rather increase your means. Review the chapter on The Money Trees in book 2 of this series and see how else you can make more money.

SELF-ASSESSMENT 4

1. Describe the 10:10:20:60 planning system, listing its advantages and disadvantages for you personally.

2. What is the importance of protection?

3. How can you make sure you stay out of debt?

Chapter 6

6. Debt Management Strategies

"Every time you borrow money, you're robbing your future self."
Nathan W. Morris

LEARNING OUTCOMES
In this chapter you will learn the following ways of DEBT REDUCTION:
- Urgent Debt
- Costly Debt
- Debt Consolidation
- Size of Debt
- How to communicate with creditors
- Debt Restructuring

When you are in debt beyond your limit, you need to do something to rescue yourself. Being overly indebted means more of your current income is going towards servicing debt, to the extent that you have little to live on. This forces you to keep borrowing just to survive. Being overly indebted also means after paying your instalments and your living expenses, you have nothing left to save. You seem to be in balance, but you are not creating a future at all.

There are a number of things you will have to do to address this.

First, make a list of all your debts, and I mean all of them, both formal and informal. We are going to look at this list from different angles, depending on how it is affecting you. Once you have this list, comb through it to determine which debts can be classified as very urgent.

Urgent Debt

Urgency is defined by asking this question: "which debt, if not paid now, is likely to cause you the most trouble?" Trouble can be defined as being black listed by the credit bureau, facing legal proceedings, facing debt collection, or facing repossession of your goods, etc. Debt becomes urgent when you neglect or are unable to make regular scheduled payments.

By separating your most urgent debt from normal debt that's on schedule, it helps you to identify the trouble spots in your relationship with debt.

It does not necessarily mean you are going to clear or pay off every debt on this sub-list. This allows you to formulate a strategy to deal with these, without neglecting the others.

The problem with urgent debt is that it may cause panic, and when people panic, they may make rushed decisions, which they might regret later.

You may need to start talking to these creditors first in order to take away your panic. If they are already upset because you have ignored them for too long, you still need to approach them and make a new offer.

It doesn't help you to rush and take another loan to pay off these urgent debts, because this new loan will be tomorrow's emergency. Your strategy for dealing with urgent debt may include:

- Consulting with a debt counsellor to

help you think through this and come up with a new plan.

- It will invariably include talking to your creditors and perhaps coming up with a new payment plan.
- It may include an assessment of some of your assets to see which you could sell to repay this debt.
- It may include a plan to make more money through an additional income stream that will be focused on repaying the arrears and eventually paying off these debts.
- It should NOT include taking another loan, unless under the advice of a trained professional. Another loan is feasible only if that loan will help you to make more money, as in a business loan. But you should not take another loan that will also depend on your salary. Don't consolidate yet. (We will talk about debt consolidation later in this chapter).

Once your most urgent debt is taken care of, that is, you have a plan for it, you should stick to your plan, and not let the other debts fall behind.

If none of your debt will put you in immediate danger, that is, you have no urgent debt, consider the next criteria of dealing with debt.

The Cost of Debt

One of the things people don't always think about is the cost of debt. There is no such thing as a free lunch. Debt comes at a cost. Now you need to arrange your debt in order, following the price of debt.

Go through your list again asking yourself: "which debts carries the highest interest charge?"

As discussed in the chapter on the four elements of debt, pay attention to the compounding interest rate. By listing your debts according to the price that you pay for your money, it helps you to figure out which debt you should try to eliminate first and save money.

A rough guide to costs in descending order would be:

- Cash loans

- Loans from micro-lenders;
- Hire-purchase agreements;
- Credit cards;
- Personal loans;
- Overdraft facilities;
- Vehicle loans;
- Mortgage bonds;
- Interest free loan from your uncle.

The above order is not cast in stone, and thus may not be true for you. You need to establish from your own records as to which debts cost you the most.

You can then devise a strategy for dealing with the most expensive debt first. With this method, you try to pay off the debt which costs you the most to have.

Unfortunately, many advisors have used this method to advice clients to roll their most expensive unsecured consumer debt into their mortgage debt.

This is a mistake because you end up paying off consumer debt over a very long period. Whatever you do, don't forget the four elements of debt.

Just because your personal loan is 30% per annum and your home loan is 11% per annum, does not mean you will reduce interest by rolling your personal loan into your home loan. If you roll your personal loan into your mortgage loan, it means you will be paying your personal loan over 25 years, or the length of your mortgage. It doesn't make sense to pay for consumables for that long. This also delays you from owning your home.

Most people, after clearing their credit card debt or personal loans into their mortgage loan, get "tempted" to use that "clean" credit card again. The lenders whose accounts have been paid off also make new offers, and people go and take another personal loan. Their situation does not improve. As we discussed under urgent debt, you can utilize anyone of those strategies to come up with extra cash to deal with your most expensive debt.

Debt Consolidation

The most frequently used methodology for dealing with debt is the Debt Consolidation method. Most debt counsellors and financiers' resort to this method in dealing with debt.

It is vitally important to make sure you know what you are doing before you engage this method.

Debt consolidation basically means you are going to borrow new money, to pay off old loans.

Why would you want to do this?

The greatest motivation for people consolidating their debt is to reduce the amount of the instalments they are paying. They also think they want to reduce the number of creditors they owe.

How does this work?

Most people look at the list of instalments they have to pay each month. They add up the total amounts of the instalments. They then focus on reducing the instalments. They generally don't think about the total debt. Just the instalments.

A debt consolidator's selling point is that you don't have to owe so many creditors. The borrower takes a fresh loan from the lender, with the goal of getting rid of all other creditors. The borrower often feels better that they only owe one creditor, instead of many.

CAUTION: The problem with this method is that IF you have not yet taken care of the habits that got you into this mess, you are very likely to get into a bigger mess than before. Many people who use their mortgage loans to consolidate their credit cards and other loans can testify to going right back to using the credit card again, or applying for a fresh personal loan.

For, as soon as your account is paid up at ABC123 Stores, you might receive a letter praising you for being such a good customer, and offering you more debt, and you might be worse off at the end. Use this method of Debt Consolidation only if you have the discipline to **not** get back into the spiral again.

Having someone you are accountable to and you discuss your finances with, might help you to stay rational, especially when those tempting offers come to you again.

Don't forget the 4 elements of debt!

When applying this method, please do not forget the four elements of debt. This is where the biggest mistakes are made. It doesn't help you to trade a cheap loan for an expensive loan.

If you don't consider interest rates and just consolidate because the lender said you qualify, you might find yourself trading a loan that you took at a lower interest rate a year or two ago, for a much more expensive loan at today's interest rates.

If you don't consider time, you could be consolidating a loan that is left with six months into a loan that will go for sixty months. Extending the time of a loan increases the amount you will repay.

Remember that debt consolidation means you are taking a fresh loan with new terms and conditions. You are selling off your "old" loans to the "new" lender. He pays off your old debt and you commit to him for another full term.

What is Debt Restructuring?

Debt restructuring is similar to debt consolidation, except in debt restructuring, you don't necessarily have to take a new loan.

You approach the current creditors and negotiate new terms with them.

If you desire to reduce the instalments you are paying, your time will obviously go up, which will affect the final amount that you owe.

You can also ask to increase the amount of your instalments. This will decrease the time you will take to repay the loan, with the effect that your principal debt is reduced.

If you should come into some extra money, or create an additional stream of income, you can use this to increase your instalments, which will get you out of debt faster.

Let us now look into how to create a debt management plan.

SELF-ASSESSMENT 5

1. What is the criterion for classifying debt as urgent debt?

2. What strategies can you employ to deal with urgent debt?

3. How do you determine the cost of your debt?

4. What is debt consolidation?

5. How should you apply the four elements of debt when you are consolidating debt?

Chapter 7

7. Debt Management Plan

"If a man works hard, the land will not be
lazy"
Chinese proverb

LEARNING OUTCOMES
In this chapter you will learn:

In this chapter you will learn:
1. The size of debt method
2. Timing in dealing with debt
3. The importance of
   communicating with your
   creditors

The idea of managing debt is about creating
a system that will guide you either out of
debt, or into using debt in a way that fits in
with your overall financial strategy.
A debt management plan is not a plan that

seems to get you out of debt overnight. It is a system that you should follow and manage over time. The best way to deal with debt is to create a strategy and implement this strategy.

Even if you are overly indebted right now, you need a strategy that will get you out of debt, and keep you out of debt. As long as you are working with debt, you are working with other people's money. The way to success in the financial game is to make sure you are growing your own money, not someone else's.

Let us look at a strategy that could help us to eliminate debt.

The Size of Debt Method

Go through that list of debt and now rearrange it according to size, from the smallest to the biggest debt. Size can be determined in two ways: either in terms of the real balance on the loan, or the amount of time left to pay off the loan.

If you follow the balance method, then you just list your debts looking at the total amount owed to each creditor.

CREDITOR	BALANCE
PAUL	1'000
PETER	3'000
MARY	5'000
ABC	10'000

If you make extra money, you use it to pay off Paul, so that you reduce the number of creditors you have.

Let us not forget that each debt is governed by the four elements of debt. Now let us look at the instalments applied to each of these, as well as the time left on each loan.

Let us assume that your smallest balance is the one with the shortest amount of time.

In other words, if you owe say 1'000 to one creditor and 5'000 to another, depending on the instalments to each, we assume that the smallest amount could be paid off first or in the shortest amount of time.

CREDITOR	BALANCE	INSTAL-MENT	TIME
PAUL	1'000	200	5 months
PETER	3'000	300	10
MARY	5'000	330	15
ABC	10'000	500	20

What this means is, in your spread sheet, slot in all the minimum payments required in each of your debts from the smallest debt to the biggest.

When you finish paying your smallest debt in five months' time as per the schedule above, instead of using that amount that used to go to your smallest debt to increase your expenses, you apply that amount in addition to your next smallest debt, which, in this case, would be to Peter.

This means you are now paying minimum debt on all your debts, except now with your current smallest debt, you are paying an additional amount, which is what you used to pay to your previous smallest debt.

In other words, even if you finish paying any of your debts as per your list, you don't change your debt ratio. If had decided that you will apply 20% of your income towards debt, you keep applying 20% of your income to debt until all your debt is paid off. All you do is you keep adjusting the amount payable to the smallest debt on your list. This encourages you as you see the list of your creditors decreasing.

Using Time as a criterion

The length of time you will take is determined by the instalments you are paying.

Obviously if your instalments to the 5'000 is 2'500 per month and your instalments to the 1'000 debt is 150 per month, you will take longer to pay off the 1'000 than you would the 5'000. So, it will take you only two instalments to get you out of the 5'000 debt and almost seven months to get you out of the 1'000 debt.

Whichever criteria you use, whether balance in amount or in time, we're trying to get you out of this debt as quickly as possible. That is the goal.

As soon as you pay off the 5'000 loan in two months, you could immediately, in the third month, clear off the balance of the 1'000 loan with the instalment that used to go to the 5'000 loan.

This is one of the most effective methods when used to eliminate debt. Listing them this way helps you to pay the smallest debt first, then using the instalment of the just cleared debt to tackle the next smallest, and so on.

Let's consider the example below:

What if you could make extra money?

If you can come up with an extra 100.00 say either from your budget or from one of your other skills preferably, then you add the 100.00 to the payment that is being made to the smallest debt on your list, which in the table below is to Paul.

CREDITOR	BALANCE	INSTAL-MENT	TIME	NEW TIME
PAUL	1'000	200	5 months	3.1
PETER	3'000	300	10	7 (3.5)
MARY	5'000	330	15	9 (3)
ABC	10'000	500	20	11 (4)

So, instead of paying Paul 200.00 and taking 5 months to repay him, you give him 300.00 and you pay him off in about 3 months.

You then take the 300.00 (that is, the 200.00 that used to go to Paul plus the new 100.00 that you are making from your other skills) and now apply it to the next smallest debt on your list, which is a debt to Peter.

Since you'd been paying Peter his minimum payment of 300.00 over the past three months, by the time you come with an extra 300.00, there will be 7 months left in his debt. You now pay Peter 600.00 instead of 300.00. In 3.5 months, you shall have cleared his debt, instead of the 7 months it would have taken, had you continued to pay only the minimum payment.

You now have access to an additional 600.00 that you can apply to your next smallest debt, which is Mary. By giving Mary 930.00 instead of 330.00 you get to pay her off in 3 months, saving yourself 6 months. You keep this up until you clear your entire list of debts.

If you focus only on the big debts, by the time you finish paying them, your smaller debts may have grown to bigger debts, or your uncle may not want to see you again. Tackling the smaller debts will free the money quickly for you to start going after the big ones. The size method is my most preferred method of debt clearance, and if applied diligently, can free you from debt in a shorter amount of time than the other methods.

Commit to Your Why

If you are not committed to your WHY, you will get back into the spiral. If you don't have a big enough reason to get out of debt and start building your financial future, you may get stuck in this habit again. It is important that you don't just want to get out of debt just for the sake of getting out of debt, you need to do it with your eye on a bigger goal. Set a vision of your future self.

Talk to Your Creditors

For any of these methods to work well however, you will have to do this seemingly daunting task: Talk to your creditors!

Creditors have better memories than debtors. Your creditors actually would like to talk to you. The reasonable ones do not mind renegotiating the terms.

Why? Well, it's certainly not because they like you or are having pity for you. They are thinking about themselves: if they can come up with a payment plan that you can afford, they are more likely to get some or all of their money back, than if they can't get hold of you.

So, don't run away, run towards them. If you are quiet, your creditors are also afraid that you will run away with their money. So, they are likely to get you in trouble. They will go to the lawyers or to debt collectors, or get you black listed with the credit bureau. And believe me, one of the assets you need to protect is your credit rating.

If you are really in trouble, be sensible and make an offer to your creditors. If they are sensible, and most are, (though sadly not all), they will accept your offer, albeit grudgingly.

Here is a sample letter you might want to send off to your creditors. But don't just send the letter and keep quiet. This sample letter is only one of the tools you might use to deal with your debt, not the answer to all your creditors. Here is the sample letter

Letter to Creditors

To: _____

Dear Sir/Madam

RE: Account number: _____

This serves as an acknowledgment of my indebtedness to you to the amount of _____

I intend to repay my full debt to you. I write to inform you that I have reviewed all my debts and after seeking advice and counselling, have come up with a repayment schedule. This will help me to fulfil my obligations to you in a way that will put me in a stable financial position.

To this end, I have created a Debt Clearance Account, made up of twenty per cent of my regular income. The purpose of this is to allow me to have sufficient resources to live on without worry or stress, and it will prevent me from going further into debt.

I am aware that as long as I continue to live on borrowed money, I don't stand a chance of ever getting out of debt and stabilizing my financial position. Each month, you will receive an amount of _____ from my Debt Clearance system until my account with you is cleared.

I am aware that this is not the amount I had previously agreed to pay you, but I'm sure you will be understanding and appreciate what I am doing. If you have any questions, please feel free to contact me. I am quite excited about my new plans and look forward to taking control of my finances.

Thank you in advance for your kind cooperation.

Yours truly,

_____

SELF-ASSESSMENT 6

1. What is the size of debt method and how does it work?

2. How do you prioritize debt based on time remaining?

3. What is the importance of making extra income in dealing with debt?

4. Why is commitment so important?

5. Why is it important to communicate with your creditors?

Chapter 8

8. The State We're In

"Debt is an opportunity for the rich"
Unknown

Most people are very much in the dark when it comes to debt. They have too much of it, and the wrong kinds. They strip their homes of equity and bounce balances from credit card to credit card to fuel their overspending. They think that because a lender is willing to give them money, they can afford to pay it back.

They focus on small things like monthly payments rather than the big picture of how the wrong kind of debt is a cancer eating away at their financial security. They pay interest year after year, enriching lenders while stealthily, silently, impoverishing themselves. And they wonder why they never seem to get ahead.

Money can buy slavery or freedom; you

choose what you buy with your money. It can buy flexibility and independence, or a prison cell. Many people have rightly observed that no matter what they do, they don't seem to be able to get out from under.

They try for several months, and once again, they find themselves right where they began. Some even pay off all their debt, but then find themselves in more debt in no time.

Is it that debt is impossible to live without or is there some magnetic pull that draws us in subconsciously?

Debt is like an addiction. One of the most effective organisations in getting people off the hook of a grossly debilitating condition of addiction is the Alcoholics Anonymous (AA) organization. Over decades now people have been able to recover from their addictions. What is the secret that the AA uses?

The AA has discovered the secret to helping people get off booze. They recognise that addiction is a spiritual problem. One of the most profound statements they make is that an addict will never be able to recover from his addiction until he changes his personality.

All human behaviours come from our beliefs.

Our beliefs sponsor our behaviours. Until you are willing to sit down and examine the beliefs you hold about money and debt, you don't stand a chance of permanent recovery from debt.

You may have many temporary recoveries over your life but a permanent recovery, which can catapult you above debt and set you in control, thus enabling you to be able to use debt to your advantage, will take your willingness to deal with your beliefs about money.

Most people never get this message. As soon as they get a job, or even before that, they get a credit card.

Instead of saving and investing, they buy stuff - usually stuff that doesn't last as long as the payments on it. If they manage to contribute to a savings or retirement policy, they either borrow from it or cash it out when they change jobs.

As their homes increase in value, they take out home-equity loans - offsetting most or the entire potential rise in their wealth with more debt.

The percentage of disposable income used to

make debt payments is now near an all-time high. The number of bankruptcies keeps setting records, with millions of people worldwide going bankrupt. Foreclosures are at modern highs, and the number of home loans more than 30 days overdue is rising.

It would be naïve to lay all the blame at the feet of consumers. Lenders have done their part by loosening loan standards and chasing after people with poor credit in an ill-fated attempt to boost their profits.

Credit-card companies ferociously battle efforts to help debtors see the hole they're digging, saying it would be "too difficult" to spell out for individual customers how long it would take to pay off their balances if only minimum payments are made.

But on a personal level, it's pointless to blame the rope salesman for selling you rope, if you use it to hang yourself. Once you've tied the noose, it's up to you to undo the knot.

Michael Masterson, author of *Automatic Wealth* wrote:

"Acknowledging and repaying your debts - these are two very fundamental requirements of integrity.

You must acknowledge your debt because it is your chance to honour your creditor. And you must repay your debt because it is your chance to honour yourself."

Chapter 9

9. How to Pay Off Your Mortgage in Record time

"Simply put, unsustainable debt is helping to keep too many poor countries and poor people in poverty"
Bill Clinton

Talking about a mortgage is not a small matter. Whole books have been written on this subject. This chapter will only focus on mortgage management plan that is necessary when you have a mortgage.

A mortgage, or a bond, is naturally a long-term commitment. You cannot treat it like you treat any other debt. It is important to understand its traits so that you have better consequence management systems in place.

What is a Mortgage?

The term mortgage, is from the French legal terms which literally means: "death pledge". The word "mort", means death, in French. And the word "gage", is from the root: "engagement".

So, when you enter into a mortgage agreement with the bank, you are entering into an "engagement until death".

Death of what?

It is obvious that the bank does not die since it is not a natural person, but a legal person. How then do you deal with a system that is set up to have you engaged until death?

You must have a comprehensive plan to manage your mortgage. Most mortgage contracts range from 20 years to 30 years.

It is impossible for anyone to predict what would happen in the twenty to thirty years while you are in this contract.

The whole contract is based on your ability to repay the loan over that period, failing which, the bank would repossess the house.

The two important questions:

In building a mortgage management plan, there are two important questions that you must address:

1. Under what circumstances could you be unable to service the loan?
2. Under what circumstances would the bank trigger the repossession clause of the contract?

The first question addresses your constant flow of income, or the availability of income for the entirety of the contract.

The second question addresses the bank' satisfaction with your repayment schedule.

Because the mortgage contract is tied to your employment contract or your ability to produce an income, those are the areas of risk that your mortgage management plan must address.

Let us answer the second question first. The bank will trigger the repossession clause under one or two of the following conditions:

1. If you should fail to service the mortgage instalment consecutively for a period of three to six months; or
2. If you should have arrears on your

mortgage equal to three to six months' worth of instalments or more. Your mortgage management plan must therefore, as a matter of principle, seek to address this by ensuring that you will not be in a position where the bank triggers the repossession clause.

Simply put, it means you should not miss three months' worth of instalments, or find yourself with arrears that would lead the bank to trigger the foreclosure clause.

Identify your risk period

Hardly anyone is hired on a permanent basis anymore. Most employment contracts have a term, often renewable, but without that guarantee.

The question is: if you lost your job today, how long would it be before you got another one?

Or, put differently: if you lost your income today, how long before you get the next income flow so that you can continue to service the loan?

That gap is your risk period, which must be

included in your mortgage management plan.

The basic plan

If, for example, your gap is six months; that is, it would take you six months between jobs, then you must save enough money to continue to service your loan while you are looking for another job.

How would you do that?

While you are continuing to pay your mortgage, you must also develop a saving plan for your risk period. You must have enough money at hand to ensure that the bank never triggers the foreclosure clause.

Most banks can help you with this. They have a mortgage savings pocket into which you can save extra money, that would be used, should you find yourself being without an income. The key is to ensure that while you still have an income, you also feed this savings pocket, also known as access bond. You must do this first, before you concoct a plan to reduce your mortgage term from say 20 years to 10 years by overpayment.

You must remember that even if you have "pushed" your mortgage by paying more into the loan, but there is still a balance, and let's say there's only 4 years left for you to clear your mortgage, if you should miss your repayments for consecutive period of three months, the bank can still trigger the foreclosure clause.

Access Bond

Word of caution about your "access bond" balance: Do not use this for anything else other than security for your risk period. Even if the bank "encourages" you to use your access bond to buy another asset or use it to pay your children' school fees, you need to remember that if you should lose an income, they will repossess your home.

Some people pay extra money into their bond account without being aware of this facility called savings pocket or access bond. You must remember that unless you communicate with the bank about your intention to save up to a certain amount in your savings pocket (for your risk period), they will put all the extra money into this account, and your 30-year term will not be altered.

To change "the contract" from 30 years to 12 years requires deliberate communication with the bank. The fact that you are paying "extra", does not automatically alter the contract. That is why the bank creates "savings pocket" or avail the access bond facility to those who pay extra but have not communicated to alter their contract.

Remember, it is not in the interest of the bank to have you pay off your mortgage earlier, because they will be losing interest. So, communication is key.

How do you pay off your mortgage in record time?

The amount of time you will take off your mortgage depends on the amount of money that you can direct towards the capital amount. The four principles of debt discussed earlier apply to this as well.

You can work with your accountant to reach your target. If you decide that you want to pay off your mortgage in twelve years instead of 20, then you need to work out how much more you need to pay in your instalments to reach that target.

Whatever you do, however, it is important to ensure that you don't go after the capital without your risk period being covered.

In fact, even the bank can help you answer that question. It is just a mathematical answer that can be calculated.

Everyone has different variables.

Once you make a decision about how much of your additional instalments should go towards your capital, you are on your way to paying off your mortgage in your own time.

Example:

> For a 1'000'000 loan over a 20-year period, at an interest rate of 10%, your monthly instalment would be 9'650,21.
>
> Should you want to reduce your period from 20 years to 12 years, all things being equal, your instalment would increase to 11'950.78; which is an additional 2'300,57.
>
> If you have identified your risk period to be 6 months, then under the 20 year deal you might need to have 57'901,26 (9'650.21 x 6) in your savings pocket or access bond to guard against the risk of you being without an income for that period.

> If you change your period, you must adjust your risk amount to 71'704,68 (11'950,78 x 6)
> Once your risk period is covered, you communicate with the bank to stop sending the additional payments to this savings pocket or access bond, but rather to address the capital amount.

The motivation for wanting to pay off your mortgage faster is obviously that you would save lots on the interest that you would otherwise pay over a longer period, and of course, you get to own your property faster. Once it's paid off, you should be careful not to treat your house as an ATM, where you withdraw the equity in your home for other projects. You would be endangering it again to the risk of foreclosure.

As you can tell, more can be said on this topic. Do your research.

Chapter 10

10. Your Borrowing Capacity

"A small debt produces a debtor, a large one, an enemy"
Publilius Syrus

Not everyone can borrow money from a bank or lending institution. The one thing that allows you to borrow money, is your capacity to repay. The larger the capacity that you have, the more money you can borrow from the bank.

There are a number of things that go into your credit score. Lenders look at your credit score before they lend you money because that determines your borrowing or repayment capacity in some form.

Your credit report is made up of your general credit history. It is built from such things as the amount of debt you're in; your repayment history; your credit mix, or the types of loans you have; and the length of that history.

The fact that you have a regular income is important, but it is also weighed against your credit score.

There are people with high incomes, but because of a bad credit score, have low or no borrowing capacity.

Your borrowing capacity is an asset even though not in a conventional way. It is an asset if you use it to your advantage, and of course it can be a liability if it is abused.

You abuse your borrowing capacity if you borrow for consumption and become a bad payer, to the extent that no one wants to lend you money.

If you use it well, however, it can help you to build your asset base or those capital-intensive investments that can produce an income for you.

Your borrowing capacity can grow as you grow, until its diminishing point, at which point it will begin to shrink as you grow older. As you build your career, say in your 30's, you might find that the banks are willing to lend you money, limited of course, by your credit score and/or your repayment capacity. When you are 30 years old, with a good credit score, the banks might be willing to lend you money for 30 years. They are willing to 'engage' with you to your retirement at 60.

At the peak of your career, say for argument's sake at the age of 45 to 50, they might be willing to lend you more money than they did when you were in your thirties, but for a much shorter time of up to ten or fifteen years.

When you are 55 years old, hardly any bank would want to lend you money for more than 5 years. They are looking at your income earning capability, which is the basis of your borrowing capacity, and they know that by age 60 you might retire and be unable to service a loan.

Beyond the age of 60, your borrowing capacity would be diminished, unless you have considerable assets that can be used as collateral.

How can you use your borrowing capacity to your advantage?

Being aware that your borrowing capacity grows, and then diminishes, allows you to figure out when the optimum time is for you to borrow money.

If you delay borrowing money for such a capital-intensive asset as a home, you might miss the boat, and not have enough time left to repay such a loan.

If you want to borrow money for a home, the optimal time to do it is most probably in your thirties and early forties.

What makes it difficult for lenders to lend you money for a home beyond the age of forty-five is that the repayments required would be very high since the repayment time would be limited to about 15 years; and the fact that at that age, your life requirements are at their highest, because you would be needing more money for your children' school fees and other life needs in general.

But of course, if you pass your affordability test, all things considered, you could still get a mortgage.

Chapter 11

11. Your Psychology of Debt

"In the long run we shall have to pay our debts at a time that may be very inconvenient for our survival"
Norbert Wiener

If you work hard, using the plans or ideas in this book, or any other idea from elsewhere to free yourself from debt, what are the chances that you might end up back in debt again?

In other words, what is the level of entanglement that you have with other people's money, that you might get knotted back into the net of debt again?

For each person there is a different answer. In determining your relationship to debt, or your psychology of debt, you need to be a great observer of your behaviour over time.

Let's start with consumer debt. I'll ask some questions and make some commentary as we go:

1. Have you ever made a determination to pay off all your credit cards?
2. Once cleared, did you ever rebuild the debt levels again?

If you determined to pay them off, but then rebuild the debt again, what does that say about your determination or your entanglement with other people's money?

What led to the repeat process of getting back into debt?

It may speak to a number of things: first, you may have paid the debt with "windfall" money, that came only once. There was no continuous income to sustain your life, so you went back into debt again.

Secondly, it may be that after clearing your debt with continues income, you adjusted your life style upwards, and therefore went back into debt to sustain the new life style.

3. Have you ever asked the bank to increase your credit card limit?

The only probing question to ask yourself about this particular move would be whether you are starting to depend on the credit card for survival, or whether it was to facilitate one special transaction, after which you got things under control again.

4. Do you have store cards with outstanding balances?
5. When you pay the instalment on your store cards, do you use the "available" balance to take new stuff from the store?
6. Do you feel that you are using your credit cards and store cards optimally and to your advantage, or do you feel taken advantage of by the bank or store or others in your circle that utilise your credit?

If you find yourself taking debt to support yourself or your loved ones, you need to assess how long that has been going on, and how much longer it can go on.

The dangers of consumer debt is that it interferes or is rather entangled with your life. The only way to separate yourself from it, is to guard your life and ensure that you only live on what you make.

Let's move on to medium term loans. These

are loans or debt that is normally payable within three to five years. These include cash loans, personal loans, car loans, or short-term asset finance such as hire purchase contracts.

1. If you have had anyone of these loans, have you ever consolidated it, and rolled it over a longer period than the initial period?

While debt consolidation may provide temporary relief by the reduction of your instalments, it is not a long-term solution to getting out of debt. In fact, it prolongs the amount of time that you will remain in debt.

Dealing with debt may be a very complex issue. Sometimes people are in debt, not because they can't afford to live debt-free, but because they have believed the lie of financial institutions that say you must have a credit score, and to do that, you must be in debt. What they are not telling you is how they benefit by you being in debt.

The Psychology of debt is deeper than the logical steps we can take to rid ourselves of debt. It is something deeper that goes into your habits and your psyche.

Most of our problems come from fear. It may

be fear of being without something, and therefore we do whatever it takes to have it, even if it means debt.

It may be fear of not being like others, and thus you go into debt to keep up appearances.

It may be fear of money itself, such that when you have it, you spend it so fast that you run out of money, and then you are forced to borrow other people's money for survival.

Whatever it may be, it is important that you identify it so that you can address it. Seeking emotional counselling may be part of the long-term solution.

Chapter 12

12. Q & A on Dealing with Personal Debt

The following answers to questions should only be regarded as a general guide and not personal advice. For a more specific advice, it would be very important to consult with a financial advisor to look at your specific situation and numbers. These however give a general understanding on some of the issues covered.

General Debt Questions

1. I Can I Borrow Money to Buy Shares?
    Yes and no. You can borrow money for anything you want. Whether or not it's a good idea to buy with the sole purpose of buying shares is another issue. The banks will not use your future shares as collateral - so the loan will be a personal loan. If you make a loss, they will not share your losses with you, you still have to pay them everything you owe them. If you make

a profit, they will also not demand your profits. So, you see, you are on our own.

2. How Does Interest Rate Affect My Loan?

Interest is the price you pay for borrowed money. It is very important to examine how this price is calculated so that you know exactly how much you are paying for your loan. There is simple interest and compound interest. They are calculated differently, and the answers will amount to different figures. The calculation of interest is also always based on the amount of time associated with your loan. This is referred to as the compounding period. Short compounding periods increases the frequency of the calculations.

3. How Does the Loan Term Affect My Loan?

- The loan term is the period over which you will repay your loan
- The longer the period, the more time the lender has to charge you interest
- The shorter the period, the shorter you have to pay interest
- The loan term will only be altered if you changed your instalment amount.
- If you increased your instalments, it will be shorter, thus saving you interest

- If you decreased your instalment, it will be longer, thus increasing the amount you owe
- When you are consolidating a loan, or doing a top-up, you are actually cancelling the old loan and starting anew one with a new loan term.
- Pay attention to your loan term because it affects the amount of money you will pay

4. How Does a Consolidation Loan Work?

- A consolidation loan is a loan you take and use to pay other loans you already have
- Most people use a consolidation loan to reduce the total amount of instalments that they pay
- By focusing only on the instalments, they take their eyes off of the amount of debt they are getting into, and they pay no attention to the amount of time they will be in debt
- Most people don't just take the amount of loan equal to the debt that they have, they take a bigger loan than the debts that they have so that they can have additional cash in their hands
- That additional cash increases the amount of their indebtedness
- Before you take a consolidation loan, it would be a good idea to meet with a

financial advisor and look purely at the numbers and their long-term implications.

5. What Are Some Advantages and Disadvantages of Debt Consolidation?

- The immediate advantage is the reduction in your instalment amount
- If you had been overcommitted, this relief can help you to rearrange your finances and take charge again
- The purpose of a consolidation loan should be to stop any other loans, especially pay-day loans that you used to survive from pay-cheque to pay-cheque
- Since your instalments get "normalised", you should not have to take another pay-day loan for survival.
- Debt consolidation should therefore only be used with the guidance of a financial advisor, and with determined financial discipline on your side.
- **The DISADVANTAGES** are that a consolidation loan increases the amount of time you will remain in debt.
- There is also the temptation to take another loan since you have a breather in your finances

- It is also important not to consolidate smaller short-term loan using the equity in your home. Don't make your house an ATM. If you do, you will end up paying for smaller things over the term of the mortgage, which is not good financial planning

6. **How Does a Change (Reduction/Increase) of My Instalment Amount Affect My Loan?**
   - Here you have to remember that every loan has 4 elements, and instalment is only just one of the four elements (The others are Interest, Time, and of course the Principal amount)
   - Any change in any of the four elements will affect the others
   - A reduction in your instalments, is made possible by an extension in the time of the loan, or technically, the starting over of a new loan term all together, as happens when you take a consolidation loan.
   - By increasing the time of the loan, you are giving interest an extra time to be charged to your principal, thus increasing your total indebtedness
   - An increase in your instalment works in your favour in that it reduces the amount of time,

and consequently, the total amount of debt you will repay.

What Is Credit Life Insurance and Its Benefits?

- Credit life insurance is an insurance policy that accompanies your loan at the bank
- It is automatically ceded to the bank and will cover the balance in your loan should you die before you finish paying off your loan
- This is a product initiated by the bank for the safety of the bank, but you get to pay the premiums on it for the duration of the loan
- If your employer is acting as a guarantor on your loan, that is, you are part of a guaranteed scheme, then credit life insurance should not be necessary, unless such things as retrenchments are not included in the policy
- So, it is important to read this policy since you are the one who is paying for it, and it is important to let your loved ones know that should you die, the loan should "settle itself"

through this policy, and the lender should not go to the employer to take your benefits for the loan

- When you take a mortgage loan, it is important to also have a credit life cover, to ensure that your loved ones don't lose the house to the lender, should you die.

Credit Cards

7. What Is the Structure of a Credit Card?

- A credit card is essentially three loans in one
- The straight credit is that which is available as "free money" for 55 days
  - o That means from the date of purchase or swiping your card, you should not be charged interest for 55 days
  - o If you paid within that 55-day period, you shall have had access to free money
- The budget facility is an instalment purchase system within the credit card

- o Whatever you charge to your budget facility, you are allowed to pay over the period that you choose, from 6 months
- Cash advance from an ATM is a loan you take from your credit card
  - o If you withdraw money from your credit card, you are essentially taking a loan from the bank

8. When Do I Get Charged Interest on My Credit Card? (Technical!!!)

- Depending on which of the facilities available on your credit card you have used, you will be charged differently
- Your straight balance does not attract interest for 55 days from the date of first usage, and technically for every 55 days from each swiping point or purchases point per transaction.
- If you don't clear your balance at the end of the month, chances are you will be caught up with interest at some point
- The purchases that go on your budget are immediately charged interest based on the term that you have chosen. There is no 55 days grace on that one.

- You will immediately be shown your total budget balance, and the instalments that will be added to your straight balance, and thus being available for clearing at the end of the month.
- If you don't clear your balance at the end of the month, and therein is your budget instalment as well, you must understand that your budget instalment will also be charged interest again, this time with the interest of the straight facility
- Cash advances at the ATM are loans and are charged immediately. They are not available for 55 days as free money.
- Cash advances will immediately reduce your straight balance, but they get charged interest immediately

9. How Does the Budget Facility on My Credit Card Work?

- The budget facility on your credit card is tantamount to an instalment sale transaction, except you don't have to fill in hire-purchase forms at the store, you already have the facility on your credit card
- You need to see these in the same light that you would a hire-purchase agreement

- If you want a big-ticket item but you don't have the money to buy it cash, you can buy it using your budget facility and pay it over the time period you choose from 6 months to maybe 48 months
- At the end of every month, the instalment amount is added to your straight balance and is available for clearance that month
- This will carry on until you finish paying the budget balance.
- Each month that you pay the instalment, that same instalment amount becomes available again in your budget balance
- So, you budget facility is part of the revolving credit, just as your straight balance is

10. What Is the Best Way to Manage and Deal with The Balance on My Credit Card?

- Managing a credit card is a matter of financial planning and financial discipline
- Because it is a revolving credit system, it is easy to not see it as debt, because every time you pay the debt, it becomes available again
- The best way to deal with a credit card is to clear the balance at the end of every month.

- If you only pay the minimum amount, you will be charged fees and interest on your balance
- It is also only better to use your credit card as available for emergencies, but not as something that you start depending on the revolving nature of the debt
- Cutting up your credit cards does not make the debt disappear, but yes it may stop you from using the physical card, even though you can still shop on line as long as you know the numbers

11. Why Do They Want Me to Pay So Little on My Credit Card?

- The required minimum payment on your credit card is not the instalment of the credit card, it is the minimum you need to pay to avoid going into default
- If you never use your credit card but only pay the minimum, you will notice that the minimum required keeps dropping each month
- If you want to pay off your credit card, you need to pay more than the minimum required on your statement,
- If you don't pay the required for one month, you might notice that the minimum doubles,

and the credit card company can suspend your credit,

- That is because you have gone into default

12. Should I Include My Credit Card Debt When I Consolidate?

- We have spoken about consolidation processes before
- Whether or not to include your credit card in your consolidation plans depends what your intentions are
- If you intend to pay it off and never use it again, then it's probably not a bad idea since credit cards carry a higher interest rates than other debt
- If however, clearing it would be creating another opportunity for you to use it, thus going further into debt, then you have to decide whether what you want to use it for is worth it or not
- It would not be a good idea to clear it only to use it further for consumption spending.
- Consolidating a credit card balance into a longer-term loan means everything you bought by that credit card is now being paid over a longer period of time

Cash Loans

13. What Is the Difference Between Formal and Informal Loans?

- There are many differences, and one of the differences is in the vetting processes
- There is usually no vetting process to get an informal loan, so you get it just for asking
- The formal loans go through a vetting process that allows you to consider whether you should get the loan or not
- The administration is also different in that there will be more formal communication with a formal loan than there would be with an informal loan
- The way the interest is calculated makes a huge difference in the pricing of these loans
  - Formal loans give you the interest rate per annum, charged monthly, which makes them generally cheaper
  - Informal loans charge you simple interest per month, and it gets compounded monthly, which makes them very expensive

- Because a formal loan follows standard pricing models, you can predict what you would owe at the end of the loan
- Informal loans can fluctuate with just one missed instalment
- Formal loans can identify how much is in arrears and you can be given an opportunity to deal with the arrears properly
- Informal loans don't separate the arrears from the normal loan, all is lumped together and can be overwhelming

14. Why Is Revolving Debt, Such as Overdraft Facilities, Credit Cards, and Cash Loans So Addictive?

- The addiction of these debts is because of the fact that they create a dependency syndrome
- Revolving debts are like a bottomless pit
- As soon as you pay an instalment, the same instalment is available again for borrowing
- Cash loans work much the same way except they are more expensive
- If you have allowed yourself to depend on the recycling debt, it is harder to get out of it
- As long as these loans are used for survival, they will remain addictive

15. What Is the Best Way to Get Out of the Cash Loan Cycle?

- The best way to get out debt is to pay and never go back
- Set up an automatic debt repayment plan and stick to it
- Cut up credit cards and never buy on line using a credit card, rather use debit cards because you can
- Don't top up any loans
- To speed up your payments, create new money and direct it towards your loans
- When you are done with loans, focus on sending money to yourself through investments
- Remember yourself
- Include yourself among those you love.
- Build your assets and your investments. That is what matters more than spending time dealing with other people's money.

ACKNOWLEDGEMENTS

The recreation of this book series was as a result of the revision of *Functional Mastery Over My Finances*. We created a course that got accredited by Botswana Qualifications Authority (BQA). We needed a more relevant "text book" that could accompany the course.

Once I had ploughed through the material, my colleague and fellow personal finance educator Poloko Mongatane was a great help in not only pushing for the accreditation of the course, but getting her hands dirty and helping to create some of the assessment questions at the end of some of the chapters, as well as doing some editing.

All this was supposed to be one big book. In fact, the paperback version remains one book divided into three parts. The book series idea however came in a bit to reduce the book to chewable chunks instead of one big bite.

Great thanks to all the people who have

given feedback since the publication of the first book in 2008. Many thanks also to all the workshop participants who brought in new perspectives on some of the concepts and for helping to improve them.

Many thanks to my staff at Moedi Financial Training for their constant support. Oteng "Owty" Orakanye, many of the workshops that have happened to improve this material would not have happened without you.

My gratitude goes to my family always for their unending support.

Thank you

Nelson Letshwene

ABOUT THE AUTHOR

Nelson Letshwene is the author of several books including *Faith and Purpose – Living Life to the full without Fear, Guilt, or Regrets.* He is also the author of *Your Longing Is Your Calling – Finding your Purpose through the seven desires of life.*

He holds a bachelors degree in business economics from The University of the Witwatersrand (Wits) (Johannesburg); an Honours degree from The University of South Africa (UNISA) (Pretoria), as well a Post Graduate Diploma in Financial Planning from Milpark Education (Cape Town)

He is a speaker on Financial and Functional literacy issues. He has written for several newspapers and magazines on personal finance issues. He has hosted several radio shows focusing on personal finance.

For more please visit his website on
www.nelsonletshwene.com

Or his Money Skills blog on

www.7moneyskills.wordpress.com
Like his facebook page:
Money Skills with Nelson Letshwene

Follow him on twitter @NelsonLetshwene

BIBLIOGRAPHY

1. Abraham Jay, 1995, 2002, 9 Pillars to business growth, Torrance, CA,Abraham Publishing group, Inc.
2. Berger Rob, Top 100 Money Quotes of all time, www.forbes.com
3. Cameron, B. 2003. Getting Started: Money Matters for Under 25s. Cape Town: Zebra Press
4. Clason George S, 1926, The Richest Man in Babylon, Penguin books
5. Griffin, G. Edward, 1994, The Creature from Jekyll Island, American Media
6. Hartmann Thom, The Last Hours of Ancient Sunlight, Three Rivers Press, NY, 2004

7. Hill, Napolean, 1937, Think and Grow Rich, Fawcett books, New York
8. Johnson, S. Et al. 1999. Saving Faith. Boston: DPI
9. Kiyosaki, R.T and Lechter, S.L 1997. Rich Dad Poor Dad, - what the rich teach their kids about money that the poor and middle class do not. New York, Warner Books Inc.
10. Kiyosaki, R.T and Lechter, S.L 1999. Cashflow Quadrant, New York, Warner Books Inc
11. Kiyosaki, R.T and Lechter, S.L 2000. Rich Dad's Guide to becoming rich, without cutting up your credit cards. New York. Warner Audio Books.

12. Kiyosaki, R.T and Lechter, S.L 2008, Increase Your Financial IQ, New York, Business Plus
13. Landsburg, Steven, E, 1993, The Armchair Economist, Simon & Schuster, London
14. Langemeier, Loral, 2005, The Millionaire Maker, McGraw-Hill
15. Langemeier, Loral, 2007, The Millionaire Maker's Guide to creating a Cash Machine for life, McGraw-Hill
16. Langemeier, Loral, 2009, Put More Cash in your Pocket: Turn what you know into dough, Harper Paperbacks
17. Lechter, M, Other People's Money, Warner Books, New York
18. Letshwene, R.N, 2008, Functional Mastery Over My Finances, Reach Publishers
19. Letshwene, R.N. 2011, Mastery Over Debt (Audio) Moedi Publishing, Gaborone
20. Masterson, M. 2005. Automatic Wealth – the 6 steps to financial independence. New Jersey: John Wiley & Sons Inc.
21. Orman, S. 2001. The Road to Wealth- a comprehensive guide to your money.
22. Orman, S. 2003. The Laws of Money, the lessons of life. New York. Simon & Schuster Inc. (Audio book)
23. Patel, Raj, 2009, The Value of Nothing, Portobello books.
24. Perkins, J. 2004. Confessions of An Economic Hit Man, Penguin Books.

25. Stanley Thomas, J, and Danko William, D, 1996, The Millionaire Next Door, Pocket Books, New York
26. Swart, N.J. 2003, Personal Financial Management, the Southern African guide to personal financial planning, 2nd Edition, Lansdowne: Juta
27. Wilde Stuart, 1989, The Trick to Money is having some!, Hay House, London
28. www.Investopedia.com
29. www.manvsdebt.com

Nelson Letshwene

RECOMMENDED READING

1. Ask and it is given, by   Esther   and Jerry Hicks (Hay House)
2. Born Rich by Bob Proctor
3. Confessions of an Economic Hit Man, by John Perkins.
4. Conversations with God , by Neale Donald Walsch
5. Personal Financial Mastery, by Nelson Letshwene (audio program)
6. Rich Dad Poor Dad, by   Robert Kiyosaki
7. The Millionaire Maker,   Loral Langemeier
8. The Millionaire Next Door, by Thomas j Stanley and William D Danko
9. The One minute millionaire, by Robert Allen & Mark Victor Hansen
10. The Richest Man in Babylon, by George Clason
11. The Science of Getting Rich, by Wallace D. Wattles
12. The Strangest Secret, by Earl Nightingale (audio program)

13.Think and Grow Rich, by Napoleon Hill

For Other Books By Nelson Letshwene

Go to:

www.amazon.com/R-Nelson-Letshwene/e/B00Q4AEMCM/ref
or scan this

THANK YOU

If you enjoyed reading this book, please feel free to leave me a review. Reviews help other readers to know the relevance of the book for them and they help authors like me to improve on our work for the benefit of our readers.

Nelson Letshwene